The Emperor of Ashes

Gaza and Beyond

Buff Whitman-Bradley

ISBN: 978-1-967022-31-1

Fomite
Burlingon, VT
fomitepress.com

The Emperor of Ashes
Gaza and Beyond

Poems by
Buff Whitman-Bradley

Enough is enough is too much

We do not mean what we say
When we say enough is enough.
What we mean to say
Is that it is all too much.

Too much stupid cruelty
Too much hatred of "the other"
Too much separating families
And throwing people in prison.

Enough is enough is too much.

Too much punching old men
Too much knocking down old women
Too much smashing windows, bashing
through doors
Too much hollow tough-guy bravado.

Enough is enough is too much.

Too much erotic attachment to weapons
Too much derision of human rights
Too much mobbing people in public places
Too much tear gas and pepper spray and
tasering.

Enough is enough is too much.

Too much making our cities more dangerous
Too much official immunity for bullying
Too much thuggery and brutality
Too much brazen lying and disfiguring of
facts.

Enough is enough is too much.

The times are ugly and dangerous

The times are ugly and dangerous.
Disagreement is a capital offense.
Strolling on official grass is punishable by
exile.

Opposing genocide will get you busted.
As will the wrong tone of voice
And the profligate use of your library card.

Learn to follow yourself home in the dark.
Hang onto your name.
The air is full of knives.

The Emperor of Ashes

It has all become ash.
That is the way he likes it,
The Emperor of Ashes.

Towns and cities and suburbs all ash.
High-tech and low-tech and no-tech
All become ash.

Great airplanes and balsa wood gliders,
Cars and bikes and scooters,
All become ash.

That is the way he likes it,
The Emperor of Devastation,
The Emperor of Ashes.

Life on Earth burnt to a crisp,
Smoldering and cindered ruins,
All become ash.

No one left to disagree with him,
To challenge him or doubt him,
The Emperor of Ashes.

He rakes through the soot to see
If he has failed to destroy anything or anyone,
The Emperor of Ashes.

He finds nothing,
Fails to hear those singing quietly
In mounds of spent coals.

Fails to note those clinging together
In small choirs of companionship,
Their music rising through smoke.

He will initially defeat himself,
The Emperor of Ashes,
And the choirs of the ash will rise.

December 26, 2025

It is late afternoon on the day after Christmas.
There is a single bird on the powerline above
the house.
It could be a phoebe, or a sparrow, or a
chickadee
But there is not enough light for me to see it
well.

It has been raining ferociously here for days
and days.
In Gaza, the winter rains are flooding the
temporary villages
Where families have put up flimsy shelters.
It is impossible to stay warm and dry.

In the West Bank, Israeli thugs continue to
commit violence
Against the property and the bodies of the
Palestinian people
Who are trying desperately to hold on to their
ancestral lands
Trying desperately to remain in their homes.

It is late afternoon on the day after Christmas.
Good Christian USA has not stopped the sale
Of deadly weapons to Israel, which continues
to use them
To maul and mangle and murder Palestinians.

It is late afternoon on the day after Christmas.
Not all children are snuggled safe in their
beds.
In Gaza children are dying of exposure and
starvation
Are dying from monstrous cruelty.

It is late afternoon on the day after Christmas.
The little bird has flown from the power line.
It is the early hours of tomorrow in Gaza
Still dark, still flooded, still waiting for the
light.

Without hands the children of Gaza
Punch the numbers into an ancient calculator
Counting the dead.

Without feet the people of Gaza
Walk every square inch of the ravage and ruin
Of their immemorial homeland.

Without homes the mothers and fathers of
Gaza
Build shelters of stories and dust
For their families to sleep in.

Without adequate defense against the ongoing
genocide
Friends and neighbors in Gaza
Disguise themselves as collapsed buildings

They hide beneath the wind
And send the jackals of shame
To howl forever in the guts of the assassins.

Without the backing of powerful nations
The Palestinian people cannot possibly
Open the monster's jaws;
The Palestinian people, nevertheless, persist.

They know how well that worked out

Have you heard?
We've scooped up another piece of ground.
Benevolent Uncle USA,
Thanks to the United Nations Security Council.
Is set to administer the protectorate of Gaza,
The Palestinian land laid waste by Israel
Over the past hundred years.
How relieved the Palestinians must feel
To have a rich and powerful uncle
Taking care of them and rebuilding their
homeland
In his own image.
How happy they must be to think of
The golf courses and luxury hotels
And Mediterranean beach clubs
And A-list shopping malls
As places that will employ them
To serve and clean up after
The wealthy clientele
Who will flock to Cote d'Gaza
In their yachts and their private jets
And helicopters
To do whatever it is the rich do
To keep them from thinking about other people.
None of this would be possible
Without the avuncular initiative
Of the United States of America.
Gaza's status as a protectorate will be familiar
To the Palestinian people.
Back in 1916 without their knowledge or
consent
Palestine became a protectorate
Of the brutal and bloody British empire,
And they know how well that worked out.

Bring flowers and food

Bring a gourmet dish
To the IDF banquet
Celebrating its glorious accomplishments
In the ongoing
War of attrition in Gaza
That has killed tens of thousands
Of Palestinian civilians
And left their homeland in ruins

Bring an iron bouquet
For every Israeli soldier
Who has shot a toddler
Through the head
Or crushed a small child
Beneath the treads
Of a monster tank.

Bring casseroles of shell casings
And steel pellets
For the Israeli platoons and battalions
Who have combed the wreckage
Of schools and hospitals
For survivors
That they can murder.

Bring chain link loaves of challah
For the Israeli pilots
Who have carpet-bombed
Acres and acres of neighborhoods
Annihilating communities
And countless lives
Believing that their holy book
Grants them permission
To commit unspeakable crimes.

Bring white phosphorous champagne
For the IDF criminals
Who have filmed themselves
Raping and murdering Palestinian women
Then proudly
And with no fear of repercussions
Posted those films
Of their sexual war crimes
On social media.

Award tin trophies and medals
To the Israeli government
And to its big brother
The fading U.S. empire
For reminding us that colonialism
And asymmetrical warfare
Are not archaic enterprises of the past
But are alive and killing
Right now.

Without them

We would like to live in a decent world.
We ask ourselves how it happens
That the people who have the power and
position
To make the world decent
Always do just the opposite.

Were they not taught about kindness
When they were children?
Did their parents neglect to mention or
demonstrate
Fairness and sharing and helping each other,
Standing up to bullies, taking responsibility
for their mistakes?

Perhaps their parents were cruel to them,
Perhaps their parents were selfish
And cared more about money and status
Then they cared about their own children,
Cared more about appearances than what lay
beneath.

If that is what their parents were
Then that is what the children learned from
their parents.
They did not learn how to give up something
for someone else.
They did not learn how to admit their
mistakes.
They did not learn how to apologize.

They did not learn how to be a true friend.
And those who cannot be true friends
Cannot be the sort of leaders
Willing to transform the systems that oppress,

Willing to create a world of justice, equality,
empathy.

It would be simplistic of course
To ascribe the cruelties of our world
Merely to bad parenting.
There is so much more that shares the blame,
Like a hole-in-the-wall gang of soulless thugs.

But it is safe to say
That those who hanker after wealth and power
above all else
Are not the generous, open-hearted ones we can
work with
To midwife a new morning into existence.
So we will go ahead and do it without them.

The beaches of the moon

We keep the meanest ones
The cruelest ones
The ones incapable of human feeling
On the beaches of the moon.

It has been this way since ancient times
This exile to the severe landscape
Of our beautiful little glowing sister
Where the banished may splash in the
petrified surf.

We watch through telescopes
To keep track of what they're up to
Watch them pummel each other
With great jagged rocks.

We watch them play king of the mountain
Atop great moonstone outcroppings
Where again and again they knock each other
off
To achieve tiny and fleeting victories.

We watch them grow old and die
Without honor, without laudatory eulogies.
We watch them decompose into space dust
And swirl into the eternal cosmos.

We are praying for the coming day
When there are no more villains to be
banished
To the beaches of the moon
And eulogies will be spoken in the language
of pure light.

I live in a country

I live in a country
Proud to invade
Proud to destroy
Proud to kidnap and murder
The leaders of other sovereign nations

I live in a country
Too brutal
Too lacking in a sense
Of our shared life on the planet
Too impatient and inarticulate
To negotiate its aims
So it vociferates instead
Using bunker-busting bombs.

I live in a country
With an embedded elite
That controls massive amounts of wealth
And leaves millions
Lacking in the wherewithal
Necessary for a decent
Productive and creative existence.

I live in a country without leaders
Only capos
Without a vision of a better world
Only hackneyed slogans
And faded old Batman comics
Without the music of hope
Only the cracked ballads of despair
Played on one-string shoebox guitars.

I live in a country
That fervently worships
Only itself

Mad with the fear
That it is rapidly losing its place
As the hegemon
A country that is
Flailing away hysterically
Demanding that the rest of the world
Keep paying tribute and obeisance
And endlessly fawning
Like a Hollywood lacky
Assuring the fading star
"You are still beautiful."

I live in a country whose mountains
And prairies and woodlands
Rivers and lakes and streams
Are beautiful
Whose ordinary citizens
Are still mostly good and kind
But whose leaders
Are a pack of craven
Crooks and scammers and parasites
Who use their positions and powers
To bully the populace
And upholster their own pockets.

I live in a country whose leaders
Make it a very difficult land
To love
But let us all keep standing
With our neighbors against
The cruelty and criminality
The self-absorption and toxic greed
That prevails in high places
And raise another banner on the flagpole
The banner of universal humanity.

Weaponized stupidity

We try to avoid the broken reasons
That litter the ground like bits of smashed
glass

The gestapo boys tell us to get out of the way
But out of the way is gone

We tell each other what we believe
As if it will shield us from what we decry

There is no help in the good, the true, the
decent
Free floating in the crying sky

Guns pointed at everyone everywhere
By adolescents play-acting manhood for each
other

Government approved murder in the streets
Weaponized, full-spectrum, top-down
dumbfuckery

From the river to the sea

A path that runs from river to sea
Worn into the soil of a captured land

The footsteps of hundreds of years
Quietly imprinting the ancestral ground

The colonial settlers say that
"From the river to the sea"

Is a war cry in the throat of violence
That must be stifled by strangulation

But those who utter the words explain
That all the land belongs to all of them

The ones who have lived there for countless
generations
And the ones who have lived there a far shorter
time

But the newer ones shout they don't believe it
Say they are in mortal danger from the native
others

"This land is only ours!" they cry
"These homes and farms and orchards are only
ours!"

How will it end?
Will there be justice?

How will it end?
Will there be sudden eruptions of kindness?

How will it end?
Will the peacemakers prevail?

Right now it doesn't look good
With daily murders of Palestinians

Right now it doesn't look good
With Israelis eyeing Iran and Syria

Right now it doesn't look good
With the settler class holding all the cards

It is difficult to imagine an end to the slaughter
It is difficult to hang onto hope

Where will we hide?

Where will we hide the children
To keep them out of harm's vicious way?

Where will we hide the helpless, the homeless,
To keep them out of harm's way?

Where will we hide the desperate immigrants
To keep them out of harm's way?

Where will we hide the infirm, the aged,
To keep them out of harm's way?

Where will we hide the confused, the
overwhelmed,
To keep them out of harm's way?

Where will we hide the snap peas
Hanging over the neighbor's fence?

Where will we hide the black-capped chickadees
Cheeping and pecking in muddy ground?

Where will we hide our venerable old owl cousins
Quietly conversing in treetops?

The goon squads and thug brigades
Are wreaking atrocity in the cities and
neighborhoods.

The bully boys and head bangers
Are pouring carnage into gutters of crimson.

The zombie camo patrols are seeking to
exterminate
Everything that matters.

Where can we hide all the people
Making the effort to care for all the people?

Let us all hide out in the open, in plain sight
Where a glittering morning sky will

Neutralize those day-blind minions
And dissolve them in whirlpools of pure light.

What will we do?

Rain thumping on our waterproof parkas
Little chunks of sky splashing into pre-
existing conditions
Crayfish swimming across muddy trails

We are weather people
Standing on promontories to keep our shoes
above and beyond
Hoping from up here to unknow what comes
next

Hearses stuck up to their elbows in gunk and
mire
People we love won't stop expiring
Like parking meters and canned peaches

Forty days and forty nights of monumental
drench
Are there any sandwiches left?
What will we do?

Sifter

I have read that the Israelis
Are harvesting body parts
From the Palestinians they have killed
And selling them for a great deal of money.

I have read that the Israelis
Are deploying state-of-the-art weapons
That completely incinerate victims
Turning them entirely to ash.

I read about a Palestinian man
Who was looking for his wife with a sifter
Hoping to find something, any small thing,
That might remain of her.

I have been sifting through my brain
Trying to find something, any small thing,
To say about these horrors beyond horror,
These acts so heinous that we are struck dumb.

I think of the boy I was,
Filled with faith in the fundamental goodness of
people,
Filled with belief that humanity
Was the moral pinnacle of God's creation.

Our children do not talk with their children
About harvesting organs from dead bodies,
About incinerating people in a flash,
But the children hear things.

So tell me please what we say to them.I do not
know.
Tell me please how to explain this profound evil.
I do not know.

I picture the Palestinian man with his sieve
Hoping to find a locket, a wedding ring
Hoping to find a hair comb, a picture frame,
But there is nothing left to find.

Shiny again

Every morning
Delivered digitally to
My deluxe telephone
I receive a comprehensive list
Of that day's words I must not say
That day's public figures
I must not criticize
That day's ideas
I must not entertain
That day's thoughts
I must not think.

I am grateful for living
In an era when such communications
Are accomplished quickly
And easily
So that I do not fall behind
Or make an unwitting error
In what political positions
I espouse
In what ideologies
And philosophies
I base my opinions upon
What candidates I root for
What comedians
I laugh at.

I know people
Who still think for themselves
Who hold contrarian views
Who speak out against
The official line.
They were my friends
But are no longer.
I abhor their heterodoxy

I condemn
Their dangerous ideas.
We must round them up
We must punish them
We must take our country back
From dissenters
And no-talent late-night talk show jabberers
And left-leaning vaccinators
And DEI dummies
And job-stealing immigrants
And Jewish antisemites
And researchers on the dole
And public media
And lgbtqi perverts
And any others we suspect of
Treacherous cogitations.
We must unite behind
Our very intelligent,
Actually the most intelligent ever
Including Abraham Lincoln,
Extremely high-IQ chief executive,
We must all be of one mind
In the same ballpark
On the same page
Polishing the American apple
With the same patriotic rag
Until we make the fatherland
Shiny again.

Guernica

I was a young man
From the heart of the Midwest
And was not long out of college
When I visited the great metropolis of New
York City
For the very first time.
I was, of course,
Thrilled with everything,
From the Met to the subways,
From the Village to Broadway.
One day I visited
The Museum of Modern Art
And spent an afternoon
Going from famous painting
To famous painting,
Probably more impressed by their fame
Than the quality of composition and brush
stroke,
And even more impressed by the fact
That just a little while ago
I was a provincial hick from Nebraska
But now I had lost my virginity
And been transformed
Into a cosmopolitan *bon vivant*
Strolling through a magnificent museum
And conversing
With some of the greatest works of art
In the world.

As closing time approached
I headed for one last gallery
And rounded the corner
Into a darkened room
With a light shining on one wall
Where a huge painting was mounted,

A black and white and gray
Explosion on canvas
Of raw, primal power
That I had read much about
And discussed in classes
And was now alone with
Face to face.
Guernica.
Picasso's response to the Nazi bombing
Of the town of Guernica
During the anti-fascist war in Spain.
A mass of bodies and body parts,
Faces contorted in mute howls,
A severed arm holding a broken sword.

Guernica:
Fascist barbarity.
Unspeakable savagery.
Horrific carnage.
Guernica:
Madness.
Depravity.
Evil.
Guernica:
Gaza.

The poor dears

The hardest to understand are not
The greedy gobblers at the top of the heap
But all those lower down
Who support their predations
And their deadly denials of resources
For the less-advantaged.
Hard to guess the source of the vitriol
That bubbles to the surface
When they talk about welfare cheats
And the scurvy homeless
And empty-eyed veterans reaching out
For spare change, a little food.
Hard, too, to figure where the rage comes
from
When they talk with such seething hatred
About LGBTQIs
And "illegals" and the lefties
Demanding a better world.

But we should waste no time
Trying to make any kind of sense
Out of these wrathful, spitting and sputtering
acolytes
Of the aristos
(Who, by the way, couldn't care less about
them).
We shouldn't try to decipher the tiny thoughts
Of these bully boys
Volunteering to work for free for the oligarchs,
Intimidating and terrorizing those
Who should be their comrades.
And we should focus instead
On building a new world community.
"The poor dears are just creeps"we should say,
"No matter how they got to be that way."

The end of the day

The stink of death suffuses the bright day
The fear of unrestrained barbarity
Wakes us early for breakfast

We will walk the kids to school
While gagging on the putrid news of war
And swallowing our own vomit rather than
telling them

We will go to work shivering
With nightmare visions of exploding hospitals
Corpses piled higher and higher

We will phone and text all day long
For the ugly headlines and updates
On the developing weather of desolation

When we return home at the end of the day
We wonder if it might actually be
The end of the day

Meanwhile in Gaza

Meanwhile in Gaza
Starvation is still the blue plate special
And whisper-thin children
Quietly endure imposed malnutrition because
What else can they do?

Meanwhile in Gaza
Parents have honed their thespian skills
Pretending that even if all is not well right now
Soon beautiful new homes will appear
Where the children will be warm and dry.

Meanwhile in Gaza
Little children with empty bellies
And heads full of the dead
Play on the ghost beaches
And in the phantom streets of absence.

Meanwhile in Gaza
Donald Trump's Peace Board
Is busily calculating the division of spoils
And working out what kind of tax to levy
So the Palestinians will pay for their own
subjugation.

Meanwhile in Gaza
There is no fuel, no power, no heat
In the flimsy tents that do not keep out the rain
That do not keep out the cold
That do not keep out the nightmares.

Meanwhile in Gaza
Three tents and two carpets make a school
A wheel-less wagon makes a public conveyance
A tightly wound bunch of rags makes a soccer
ball
And a child with no hands plays goalie.

So many good people
                    -Minneapolis, January 2026

So many good people are standing
Against the authoritarian power grab
Occurring now in the cities and suburbs
Occurring now in the chambers and corridors
of dominion.

So many good people standing
In rain and snow, in harm's way,
To protest the gangland takeover
Of the three branches of government.

So many good lawyers filing class action
lawsuits,
Defending activists wrongfully accused,
Defending migrants seeking a decent life,
Defending whistleblowers who reveal plans to
seize the gears.

So many good parents standing
On street corners, in front of schools and
government buildings,
Carrying signs and banners, singing songs of
hope,
Hope for their kids, hope for the future.

So many good neighbors standing
In front yards, on porches, in driveways,
Practicing the politics of connection,
Letting each other know that they matter.

With thanks to the publications where many
of these poems first appeared: *Dissident Voice,
New Verse News, Turtle Island Poetry*

9 781967 022311